A Heart
Full of
Love

ISBN 0-935906-02-9

A Heart Full Of Love

Javan

This book is written

For those willing to pay the price
To learn the meaning of Life -
And to know the joy of Love

Once upon a time...
There was a Heart

Life is a time for learning.
We must learn that our Life is as important
as that of any other person on Earth,
but never more important. We must learn
that we have every right to Happiness,
yet it is up to us to find and recognize it.
We must learn that Life is not easy
nor is it permanent, others will come and go,
and often their departure will cause us pain.
We must learn to develop a positive attitude
that can handle Life's disappointments.
And we must learn that in order to find Love,
we must look inside our own Heart.
For if we can't find it within,
we will never find it without.

I think I would rather possess
Eyes that know no sight
Ears that know no sound
Hands that know no touch
Than a Heart
That knows no Love

I will know Love
No matter what circumstances
The World may give me
No matter how many people
Choose to turn and walk away

I will find Love
In the laughter of little children
In the gentleness of animals
In the beauty and glory of Nature
In the knowledge of myself

And when the day comes
That I find someone who does not turn away
I will give Love
With all my Heart

We must realize
That even in the middle
Of all the World's humanity
We are still individuals
And for the most part
We must stand alone

If I stand alone
It does not mean
I am any less a Human
If my arms do not hold another
It does not mean
They are incapable of holding
If my tongue is silent
And never speaks the words of Love
It does not mean
That it will be mute
When the time comes
That the words can sincerely be spoken

And just because the World
Has not yet introduced
The one that will share my Life
It certainly does not mean
That I am incapable
Of Loving

I think the loneliest moments
That my Life has ever known
Took place in the middle of a crowd
While seeking someone
I could relate to

There is Someone Special
In this World for me
For that's the way I believe
It was meant to be

So I search every face
In the crowd I see
For there is Someone Special
In this World for me
And the only reason I can think of
That she's not here with me
Is she must have turned left
At Albuquerque

And into this Heart
   Were dropped the seeds of
      Affection, Understanding, Compassion

Teach Me
To see the World in a different Light
The Light of your Love

Help Me
To learn to cherish each new day
And all the Opportunities that it brings

Give Me
The Strength to handle Life's problems
Knowing that you are beside me

Let Me
Be comfortable in the Knowledge
That since you have come into my Life
I will never walk alone

There was a time
When my mind had its Freedom
To wander aimlessly through the days
To travel to distant Lands
Or soar among the clouds
And to hold imaginary Lovers
Through the night
But now things have changed
And it seems my mind has been tethered
And can never get too far
From thoughts of you

When I take stock
Of all the times we shared
Strangely enough
The memories I hold most dear
Are not from the moments of fun and laughter
But of the times
When food was scarce and times were tough
And you found your strength in me
And I in you
For surely those were the times
That we truly learned the meaning
Of Love

The seeds took root
    And the Heart was filled with Beauty

From another Land
You came to me
A Land of peace and quiet
And serenity
You wiped my brow
And held my hand
And taught me the ways
Of your own Land
And even though now
You have slipped from me
I still know the peace and quiet
And serenity

It is hard
  To be strong
    When Someone Special
      Leaves your life

  And it doesn't
    Get any easier
      With practice

Where will I go
When there's no where to go
But away from you

What will I say
When everything's been said
But we're through

What lies ahead
When it all lies behind
But the memories

Will I have the strength
To wipe the tear from my eye
To give one last hug
And whisper "good-bye"

But Life can frequently be difficult
Especially for such a fragile Heart

Anyone who is willing to listen
Can hear what is being said
Even when no words
Are being spoken

If only
I had learned to speak
A little more softly

If only
I had learned to listen
A little more carefully

If only
I had held her
A little more often

If only
I had tried to be for her
What she was trying so hard
To be for me

Maybe I wouldn't be alone
Wondering
If only

I guess I'll never forget the feeling
For I've known it so many times before
When you said you needed to be honest
And that there was someone else
Also in your life
Then you smiled and held my hand
And assured me that it would never affect
The way you felt toward me

And as you walked away
I realized
We human beings have developed
Some very strange ways
Of saying "goodbye"

Have you ever noticed

That the words…

"Goodbye"

"I'm sorry"

"I love you"

Are so easy to pronounce

…Yet so hard to say

And sometimes it was bruised

If you can just turn
And walk away
And feel there's nothing more
You need to say
And you do not feel a tearing
In your Heart

If you can so easily
Forget about me
And all the things
I tried to be
Then I guess there was really no reason
For you to stay

It hurts
To see you walk away
For admit it or not
You were an important part of my Life
And the time we shared
Will forever be a part of me
So even though I realize
That it was never meant to be
Still
It hurts

Love can sometimes be like Magic
But Magic can sometimes…
just be Illusion

And a few times
It was even broken

I don't think it was selfish
That I wanted to be with you
That I wanted to share your laughter
That I wanted to protect you from your fears
That I wanted to be a part of your Life

But I admit I had my needs
I needed understanding
I needed someone to hold
I needed someone to talk to

For you can only hold a pillow
For so long
And there's only so much you can say
To a dog

You might have loved me
If you had known me
If you had ever known my mind
If you would have walked
Through my Dreams and Memories
Who knows what Treasures
You might have found
Yes, you might have loved me
If you had known me
If you had only
Taken the time

Watching you walk out of my Life
Does not make me bitter
Or cynical about Love
But rather makes me realize
That if I wanted so much
To be with the wrong person
How beautiful it will be
When the right one comes along

We not only learn from our Mistakes
But we also pay for them
And when we do not learn from them
We frequently wind up paying twice

But time healed the wounds
And its Beauty increased

And so it is
That now I've learned
It's possible to laugh
With a lump in your throat
And tears can be hidden
If you really try
And the roles we people play
Would earn more Academy Awards
Than the screen ever knew

Can it be
That I am a stranger
Even to myself

Can it be
That I thought I was someone
While everyone else knew different

And is it possible to wear a mask
That hides the truth
Even from ourselves

And if this be the case
Is there a way to learn
How to shed the mask
And face the truth

Today someone asked
If I would like to be able to go back
And change all the things that had gone wrong
In my Life
And although at first
The idea seemed rather appealing
I quickly realized
That the good and the bad are so intertwined
That I couldn't change part
Without changing the whole

From time to time
Through the years
The World has brought me down
To teach me about pain
And has filled my eyes with tears
But there came a day
That I started to understand
That it is not about pain
That the World is trying to teach me
But rather about Life
And the not so simple act
Of Being Human

We must realize
That in the realm of Mankind
There are no kings, queens, or presidents
No judges, officers, doctors, preachers, or teachers
Not even fathers, mothers, daughters, or sons
There are only Human Beings
Who wear these titles
And no matter what title
A person may wear
From time to time
He or she will make
Some very
Human Mistakes

A grain of sand is no greater or lesser
Because of its position on the beach
In the end it is still...
Just a grain of sand

A child does not have to be taught
How to be happy
Or the ways of Love

It is fear, hatred, and prejudice
That have to be taught

And from the condition of the World
We can see
That unfortunately
There are some very good teachers

What greater Lesson
Can a Human Being learn
Than to guide his words and actions
To be considerate
Of the needs and feelings
Of all the other occupants
Of this World

If I am truly honest
I can not say Suffer Love
To every stranger I meet
For then what would I offer
To those truly special in my Life

Instead, I would like to believe
I offer

Understanding
That their Life is as important to them
As mine is to me

Compassion
For all the pain and suffering
That comes with being Human

Tolerance
Of that which they choose to believe
And the way they choose to live

And the Freedom
To know their own Life
And to discover and develop their own abilities
Without any unwarranted hatred or prejudice from me

For even if I do not offer Love
There is no other foundation
On which Love can grow

And the Heart found true Happiness
Came when sharing with others

Just how high
Can the Human Heart rise
In a World so full of uncaring eyes
Where Animals suffer and Children die
And people fight Wars without knowing why
Where alcohol and drugs cause wasted lives
And shelters are full of unwed mothers and battered wives

But should the day come that man learns to care
And no longer wants just to take, but also to share
And he learns that everything has the right to live
And Life is something he can take, but can not give
When he learns to approach Life with a Heart full of Love
For everything on Earth and in the Heavens above
When he learns to do these things
He will have opened the door
To knowing just how high
The Human Heart can soar

I often wonder
If I am the man
That I would be

If I were a boy
Dreaming of the man
That I would be

If my Life is to travel smoothly
Then I must give it a sense of direction
I must take out the charts
And plot my own course
For Life is too short to wander aimlessly
And hope by chance to find my goal
And I must be willing to pay all the Tolls
That are exacted along Life's Highway

For then and only then
Will I be permitted
To reach my final destination

If we are born with Beauty
We owe a debt of gratitude to the World
But if we die with Beauty
The World owes a debt to us

Death is not the Opposite of Life
It is a part of Life
A part we've not yet explored
And thus do not understand
And it is only natural
To fear what we do not understand
But with the right attitude
We can make Life beautiful
With this same attitude
Can Death not be the same

*Yet, no matter how much it gave
There was always more*

Maybe I didn't solve
Any of the World's problems today
But I did try to conduct my Life
In such a way
That I did not add to them

If I should come out ahead
At the end of this game called Life
It won't be because of my fancy style
Or that I knew how to play it so well
But more because I just kept getting up
And plodding along
Till the World finally just got tired
Of knocking me down

If it's just a Game
That we play
Before we leave this Earth
For the Heavens above
Then surely the one who wins
Is the one who learns
How to have
A Life full of Living
And a Heart full of Love

Javan (which is the author's given middle name) was born October 19, 1946 in a small North Carolina town. He lived in N.C. through high school and college, then moved to Atlanta in 1968, where he worked as an agent for Eastern Airlines until the end of 1977. In 1979 Javan self-published his first book and started traveling around the country with his golden retriever puppy, Brandon, introducing the book to bookstores. There are four titles now available and Javan still travels frequently both nationally and internationally.

Unfortunately, Brandon died in 1988.

Now you can visit Javan at
www.javanpress.com
effective May 1, 1998

There are four titles from Javan available
in a matched set:
Footprints In The Mind
Meet Me Halfway
Something To Someone
A Heart Full Of Love
Many bookstores are now stocking these books;
however, nearly all general interest bookstores
have them available from their distributor
and can get them in a few days.

We must accept the fact that Life is ever changing, and the people, pets, and possessions that are in our life today may be gone tomorrow. Although it is painful when this happens, we must find the strength to continue with our life. And we must learn that at times like these the more we care about others and their problems, the quicker our problems will diminish.

Now I would like to close by thanking you for the time we've shared. I hope your problems will be few and your courage strong, and most of all I wish for you "a life full of living and a heart full of love".

Sincerely,

Javan

To Brandon
(November 1978 - October 1988)
For all the time we shared
And all the love you gave

Now each night
Wherever I am
I think of you
Wherever you are
And in my heart I repeat
"Thank you"

from <u>Footprints In The Mind</u>

Brandon and Javan

1983 publicity photo

I would like to take a moment and say thank you to Brevard College and the faculty and staff that helped make my stay there enjoyable and meaningful. Brevard is a wonderful small college that is located in a beautiful, peaceful setting in the mountains of North Carolina. When I attended it was exclusively a two-year college, but it has grown considerably and now offers not only the two year degree, but also several four year degrees. Any student seeking an excellent yet reasonably priced education in a beautiful environment should consider taking a look at what Brevard has to offer.

For you just can't empty
A Heart Full Of Love

Before we part I would like to remind you that it is not the things that happen to us that determine the quality of our life, it is strictly our attitude toward the things that happen. We can not control what other people say and do, we can only control ourselves. Therefore, we must concentrate on "Knowing Ourselves", who we are, what our abilities are, and what we want to do with our life. We must have our dreams and the courage to pursue them, while respecting the right of others to do the same.